Weathering
the Storm

The Lessons Learned Series

Learn how the most accomplished leaders from around the globe have tackled their toughest challenges in the Harvard Business Press *Lessons Learned* series.

Concise and engaging, each volume in this series offers fourteen insightful essays by top leaders in industry, the public sector, and academia on the most pressing issues they've faced. The *Lessons Learned* series also offers all of the lessons in their original video format, free bonus videos, and other exclusive features on the 50 Lessons companion Web site www.50lessons.com/storm.

Both in print and online, *Lessons Learned* contributors share surprisingly personal and insightful anecdotes and offer authoritative and practical advice drawn from their years of hard-won experience.

A crucial resource for today's busy executive, *Lessons Learned* gives you instant access to the wisdom and expertise of the world's most talented leaders.

Other books in the series:

Weathering the Storm

LES50NS
www.50lessons.com/storm
Boston, Massachusetts

Printed in the United States of America
13 12 11 10 09   5 4 3 2 1

Library of Congress Cataloging-in-Publication Data

Weathering the storm.
        p. cm. — (Lessons learned)
    ISBN 978-1-4221-3979-0 (pbk.)
    1.   Management. 2.   Business cycles. I.   Harvard
Business School. Press.
    HD31.W356 2009
    658.4'012—dc22

                                        2009014936

In partnership with 50 Lessons, a leading provider of digital media content, Harvard Business Press is pleased to offer *Lessons Learned*, a book series that showcases the trusted voices of the world's most experienced leaders. Through personal storytelling, each book in this series presents the accumulated wisdom of some of the world's best-known experts and offers insights into how these individuals think, approach new challenges, and use hard-won lessons from experience to shape their leadership philosophies. Organized thematically according to the topics at the top of managers' agendas—leadership, change management, entrepreneurship, innovation, and strategy, to name a few—each book draws from 50 Lessons' extensive video library of interviews with CEOs and other thought leaders. Here, the world's leading senior

A Note from the Publisher

executives, academics, and business thinkers speak directly and candidly about their triumphs and defeats. Taken together, these powerful stories offer the advice you'll need to take on tomorrow's challenges.

As you read this book, we encourage you to visit www.50lessons.com/storm to view videos of these lessons as well as additional bonus material on this topic. You'll find not only new ways of looking at the world, but also the tried-and-true advice you need to illuminate the path forward.

⊰ CONTENTS ⊱

Contents

If you knew that the crisis you're facing today would transform your career and revolutionize the way you do business, would you be ready for the challenge?

In this book, extraordinary leaders share their hard-won secrets for survival in the perfect storm and how these changed their lives and companies. When the going gets tough, the tough *reinvent themselves*, and this book is your personal, one-on-one power lunch with executives who never give up.

It's not that great managers are bullet-proof or impervious to pain. "Life was grim. Everyone was pessimistic. I used to have this recurring nightmare, seriously, that I got to the office one morning and all the clients had left and all the people had left. And I was all alone in this place," admits Shelly Lazarus, Chairman & CEO, Ogilvy & Mather Worldwide. "So, what do you do? You turn the lights out. But the truth was that everyone had their résumés on the street, and all the clients were wondering whether they should stay at Ogilvy, because it was falling apart."

Weathering the storm wasn't any easier for Richard Santulli, Chairman and CEO of NetJets: "We were basically broke. I had personally guaranteed all the debt, which my attorneys told me I should not have done. I said, if the company failed, I should fail, too. And the lenders respected me for that."

We'll show you how all of the executives you'll meet in this book ultimately achieved extraordinary success, but not until they had first pulled their companies from the brink of disaster. "I felt a profound sense of failure" when the company was running out of cash, says Ping Fu, Chairman, President and CEO of Geomagic. "That was my first reaction. The second was fear. Oh my God, I raised the money; my own money, my family's and friends' money, the investors' money. *They trusted me.* Now I had to tell them that their money was down the drain and that they didn't have a job. I panicked."

Foreword

In this book, you will get the inside scoop on how these battle-scarred leaders overcame their fears and took swift action to pull their firms from the precipice. You will get brutally frank advice about how great managers must get out of their own way, outlast their competition, turn their companies around, and, most importantly, keep their heads while everyone else is losing theirs.

"We had people standing up and screaming at the management team [at the shareowner meeting], calling us names which I won't repeat," recalls Erroll Davis Jr., former Chairman of Alliant Energy Corporation. It was the height of the energy crisis and Enron scandal.

"Don't run away from it, or try to blame the economy or any other exogenous variables," Davis advises. "You learn a lot about yourself and your management team in the middle of a crisis. You learn the depths of people's emotions. You learn that you have to make tough decisions quickly. You learn that you have to figure out new ways to motivate people when your standard economic motivations are no longer there. You have to suggest to them that they are part of building something of which ultimately they will be proud."

This book tells you how. You'll hear the hard facts about what it takes to persevere in the worst of circumstances and how managing the crisis you face today can transform your organization and promote your career in ways that will pay dividends for years to come.

—Mark Thompson
Bestselling coauthor of *Success Built to Last*

Weathering
the Storm

Be Prepared for Adverse Business Conditions

J. W. Marriott Jr.

Chairman and CEO, Marriott International

WE ALL KNOW THAT no tree grows to the sky, and that business downturns are always going to be with us. The age of technology is wonderful, but it cannot guarantee against downturns and adverse business conditions, which are almost always caused by things beyond our control. So it's important to prepare for them, be ready for them, have your house in order, and never overextend yourself.

Back in the late 1970s, we decided that we were going to be a management company and not a hotel ownership company, so we sold the group of hotels that we owned and took back management contracts. We continued to use our brands and managed the business, but we did not own the real estate. We decided we could make a better management contract if we owned the real estate, built it, and then sold it to another owner and took back the contract rather than have somebody else develop it for us. So we were actually building hotels for sale.

And so all through the 1980s we were building and selling hotels; we sold probably anywhere from $15 to $20 billion worth of hotels. Then we got up to around 1989, and we had $3 billion worth of hotels on our books for sale. We had buyers lined up for all those hotels, and the real estate market crashed in 1989–1990.

Be Prepared for Adverse Business

All of a sudden, we were in a recession. And all of a sudden, we had a war in the Gulf. So we had a war; we had a recession; and we had too much real estate on our books, too much debt. We had to scramble to figure out what to do. We sold off some of the hotels and took back the contracts, but we were unable to get rid of all of them; we still had a lot.

So we spun off the management part of the business into a new company, and we left the hotels and the debt with the hotels back in another company. These were very trying times for us, very difficult times, but we came through because we stuck to the plan, which was eventually not to own hotels but to manage them.

The lesson learned here is that no tree grows to the sky. We thought that we could do this forever, and we overextended ourselves. I think the most important thing is: be careful as you go along, make sure that your plan is being executed, and don't get out ahead of yourself. Realize that it's not always going to be sunshine up above.

Weathering the Storm

There will always be some clouds coming over—and when the clouds come over, you have to be ready for them.

TAKEAWAYS

- The age of technology cannot guarantee against downturns and adverse business conditions, which are almost always caused by things beyond our control.

- Stick to your original plans to successfully weather difficult times.

- Take care to ensure that your plan is being executed, and don't get out ahead of yourself.

Weathering the Perfect Storm

William Harrison

Former Chairman, Director, and CEO,
JPMorgan Chase & Co.

IN MY THIRTY-EIGHT-YEAR career,
I've had a lot of challenges. It's not always
easy to figure which was the greatest, but
the one I would cite is a time after the
JP Morgan-Chase merger in 2000. The
reason is because mergers are very hard.

Weathering the Storm

I've been through three major mergers of
the big New York banks, and they're tough.
They're the ultimate test of leadership, because in a merger, things are moving so fast.
Your leaders can only put you in a job; they
can't command that everybody respect you.
And in a merger environment, it's a real
democracy. If you're not doing a good job
as a leader, you get exposed very quickly.
Having been through all of these and having
survived, I felt that I'd taken on most leadership challenges that I could ever think
about, and I'd done them okay.

So it was a year after the J.P. Morgan &
Co.–Chase Manhattan Bank merger. That
merger had gone relatively well. We were
doing well, and all of a sudden the perfect
storm hit. And the perfect storm was the
aftereffects of the bursting of the bubble
in the 1990s played out to the marketplace—
and to us specifically as a firm in three
very specific ways: we had a significant loss
in our private equity portfolio; we had
significant losses in our lending portfolio
because of the telecom media space; and,

unfortunately, we'd had major relationships with Enron and WorldCom that resulted in both financial and reputational damage to the firm.

All of that hit at one time. It was a whole new set of challenges, because it wasn't just financial; it was a regulatory challenge for us. The press loves to take on things like this, so we became the lightning rod. Everybody, it seemed, was on our case. It was the perfect storm. Here I had been thinking a year or so before that I couldn't have any more real leadership challenges. Well, guess what? I had a new one, and it was very different and very tough.

Some of the lessons I learned are that when you get into some new, really tough challenge, you have to do several things. You have to stay calm, you have to keep things in perspective, and you have to stay balanced. Now, that's easier said than done, but I think I was able to do it, and it had a big impact on all of our people.

Second, you have to then lay out—to the firm, to your people, and to your other constituents—a vision. Remind people who you are. Remind people what the strategy is. Remind people that, yes, we are going through a challenging time, but we have a lot of great strengths, and we're going to do just fine. And in my heart of hearts, I absolutely believed that. I had no concern that JPMorgan Chase was going to do anything other than come through this, maybe even as a better firm. You just have to do the best you can do.

People walked into my office and said, "Bill, you know, jeez. I'm sorry this has happened to you personally, that you're having to manage all this. I know it's really hard. I don't know how you're doing it."

I said, "Look, on a personal side, let me just put this in perspective for you. The worst thing that can happen to me is that I lose my job. And if I lose my job, I'll be sad. I'll be disappointed. But it's not the end of the world, because I'm doing the best job I can. I'm healthy, I have a great family at home, and I've had a very fortunate life. So I'm not going to feel sorry for myself.

I'm just going to take the positives and go do the best job I can."

When you do the best you can, you find out that you can do a lot better job than you probably think you can when you're faced with a problem, with a challenge. When I added all of that up, it was a major challenge, but I did some of the things I talked about, and we came through that. I learned a lot from it; I'm a much better leader today having been through that.

TAKEAWAYS

- ⇥ When you encounter a new, difficult challenge, stay calm, keep things in perspective, and stay balanced.

- ⇥ As you weather challenges, remind the firm, your people, and your

Weathering the Storm

constituents what the business, the strategy, and your strengths are.

- ⚐ A leader must have strong personal belief in successful, positive outcomes to challenging times in order to reassure the people he leads.

Managing Through a Crisis

Erroll Davis Jr.

Former Chairman, Alliant Energy

THE IMPACT OF ENRON and its associated crisis on corporate America—and particularly on the energy industry—cannot be underestimated. We were a company formed in 1998 by a three-way merger between three utility companies. We were implementing our strategic plan, and things were going well for us until the Enron crisis came—followed by the Arthur Andersen meltdown, followed by the trading crisis in California.

In 2002, particularly in the second half, the entire energy market went into meltdown. We had a liquidity crisis, stock prices dropped precipitously—ours dropped by about 40 percent—and we had a number of minor liquidity challenges in the fourth quarter. These were tough times. When we analyzed what we did, we came to the conclusion that, strategically, we had taken pretty much the right steps. We had been doing the right things. But bad things often happen to good people because of strategies they have adopted.

We also learned a lot about managing under crisis. I think 2002–2003 was the first down business cycle in the electrical utility industry ever, and many of us learned a lot during that period. One of the things we learned about managing under crisis was, first, to stay calm. Second, don't look back. Figure out what you have to do, commit to doing it, and be accountable for putting in place the strategies that got you where you are. This can be particularly painful. For example, we had to cut our dividend by 50 percent. The subsequent shareowner meeting in 2003 was not a very pleasant experience. We had people standing up and screaming at the management team, calling us names, which I won't repeat, or referring to certain lineages, which I also won't repeat. But that's to be expected; you learn the depths of people's emotions about their investments. It also makes you aware that you've been entrusted with their capital, and you have to produce a return on that.

You learn a lot of things in the middle of a crisis. You learn a lot about yourself and your management team. Those who you thought you could depend on you learn that you can't, while people you thought were strong turn out to be less strong. These are great learning experiences, and I think it helps you build stronger teams as you go forward.

You learn that you have to make tough decisions quickly. You also learn that you have to figure out new ways to motivate people when your standard economic motivations are no longer there. You have to start to suggest to them that they are part of a resurrection program; they're building something of which ultimately they will be proud. Again, one of the primary lessons is about being accountable: you adopted the strategies that put you where you are; accept that.

Certainly don't run away from it, or try to blame the economy, or Enron, or any other exogenous variables. They're there: they contribute, but you're responsible for identifying and mitigating the risk, and for working a way out of negative situations. If you act as if you know what you want to do and that you're determined to do it, you will find that there will be people who will stand beside you and behind you and follow you in that process.

TAKEAWAYS

⚔ When managing under crisis stay calm, don't look back, make tough decisions quickly, and be accountable for putting in place the strategies that got you where you are.

⚔ You can learn a lot about yourself and your team when a crisis arises to test your strengths and assumptions.

⚔ If you act as if you know what you want to do and that you're determined to do it, people will stand beside and behind you and follow you in that process.

The Self-Reliant Leader

Sir Michael Rake

Chairman, BT Group

I THINK ONE OF THE things that,
fortunately, I experienced very early in
management was the question of learning
to be self-reliant and resilient. I think this
is critically important to learn at a young age
because if you don't, when you come to the
top of an organization—particularly a large
one—you're in quite a lonely position and

you continuously need to reflect confidence. You need to reflect something that your people understand and have confidence in.

For me I think it goes back to 1986 when I was asked by the firm to go to the Middle East. At that time the Iran-Iraq war was on, and there were huge financial crises in the banking sector. In a matter of days, I found out that we had a lot of difficulties in our business there. Two or three of our people were under investigation by the judicial authorities, we didn't have enough cash to pay the wages at the end of the month, and I think the day after I'd been told this, we lost a client that provided about 30 percent of our revenues.

I remember calling my boss in London and telling him that there were slight problems here with these three people under investigation, having lost 30 percent of our revenues, and not having enough money to pay the wages at the end of the month. He said, "Well, good luck, Mike." It was a very good lesson; we went from really near-collapse and catastrophe to getting a group of people together and realizing we had to deal with it.

We had a very difficult eighteen to twenty months, but within two years we'd recovered all of our market position, we were highly profitable, we were remitting profits back to the head office, and people were willing and keen to join us. Our reputation had been fully established again in the marketplace.

This happened because we needed to be pretty tough about it and recognize we had no choice, but also because I think people had confidence—even though I wasn't quite sure what the hell I was going to do. The fact that people had confidence meant the team really got together and suddenly realized that we had to find a solution because no one was going to help us. We might as well get out there and do something about it—so we really fought back. Whereas it appeared that everything was against us at the beginning, step-by-step we dealt with one thing, then another, then another. If you work hard enough at it, you suddenly find that maybe you get a bit of good luck too, and it starts to go in your direction.

Learning to deal with those issues, learning that there is no escape but having to deal with it yourself, realizing that you had to motivate people to work with you to find solutions, and being absolutely determined—because you have no choice but to deal with that problem—is an enormously important lesson. And the younger you learn it, the better for you.

What you need to do in a leadership position is to actually ensure that the people you're developing within an organization are given experiences that will make them self-reliant, where they have to learn to depend on themselves, where they actually have to learn. In whatever business you're in—whether you're a doctor or you're running an accounting practice or a FTSE 100 company—there are times when things go wrong. You tend to get the bad news, and things go wrong.

Learn to be able to deal with and absorb bad news and be able to turn it around.

Find out what you can do: What are the good things? What are the silver linings within that particular cloud? How you react to that situation is critically important to the people around you, how the organization sees you, and therefore how the organization responds to that particular crisis. If you start getting downcast or getting depressed, then you have grave difficulty in bringing your people with you.

TAKEAWAYS

⚔ Accepting that there is no escape but having to deal with a crisis yourself, realizing that you have to motivate people to work with you to find solutions to that crisis, and becoming absolutely determined to persevere are important lessons to learn early in your career.

Weathering the Storm

⚔ Leaders need to ensure that the people they're developing are given experiences that will make them self-reliant, that will teach them to depend on themselves.

⚔ How leaders respond to bad news and difficult situations is critically important to the people around them, how the organization sees them, and therefore how the organization responds to any particular crisis.

———◆◆◆———

Work On What You Can Control

Sir Nick Scheele

Former President and CEO, Ford Motor Company

———◆◆◆———

I BECAME PRESIDENT of Ford of
Mexico, and Mexico had gone through
a difficult period—i.e. huge inflation of
2000 percent per year—and everybody was
concentrated on the effects of inflation and
what they could do to control it in the business. It had some dramatic negative results
because with inflation came devaluation of

the peso, parts were being imported from the United States, and there was also price control so you couldn't increase the prices to recover the devaluation losses. There were negative results for everybody in the industry, and it was a very difficult period.

When I got there, we were in a loss situation. The economy was poor, sales were down, we were on low-time working—we were, in fact, only working about three days a week. Not very good.

But people were constantly in meetings saying, "What can we do about the inflation problem, what's the forecast for next month, and what can we do about it?"

And I said, "Well, you know, we don't know what the inflation's going to be—we don't control inflation. That's really going to be an outcome of government policy and market belief in where the peso is going in relation, in this case, to the dollar.

"But there are many, many things that we can influence, that we control directly—like the quality of our vehicles, the productivity of all of us in the offices as well as in the

factories. We can control the desirability
of our cars. Do we have the right colors,
the right features? Do people want to buy
the cars? If we work on the things that we
can control, isn't that going to give a more
meaningful result?"

So we started working on the things that
we could influence and control. The government that came to power in Mexico in
December 1988, they really started turning
things around. It wasn't quick and it wasn't
easy, but by the spring of 1989 you could
see a significant improvement in consumer
confidence, in inflation and, in conse-
quence, in devaluation. And then very
quickly it happened; it all came under
control.

We were poised. We were ready to respond because now the marketplace started
requiring more vehicles. And we were ready
with those vehicles. We were ready with cost-
effective vehicles and ones that people actually wanted to buy. We hadn't been working
on things that we couldn't possibly control
or indeed even influence. Our competitors

had. So we were in a position to respond much more quickly.

As a result, in 1989 we had a record year in Ford of Mexico's history, and it was very profitable. We gained market share. We also saw that our dealers were profitable. And, more importantly perhaps, we saw that our customers were very satisfied with the vehicles that they bought, as they were actually vehicles they wanted to buy because they matched their needs. Ultimately, that is clearly the best market proposition to have.

It was a very good time for me to be in Mexico. It was a great time to learn general management. It was also a great time to realize that you should be working on the things that you can influence and control, not on other things where you're really only doing busywork because whatever you do won't change the outcome. Out of that I learned some pretty important lessons.

Only work on things that you can control, and let the rest happen. Search and work on things where you can influence the outcome. As you work on them, work on

making sure that you're the best in class.
That means knowing how good your
competitors are, matching and beating
them, and then you can be in a position
to respond when conditions change. Being
ready is perhaps more important than anything else. If you're not ready and you miss
the opportunity, it tends not to come
around again.

TAKEAWAYS

⊣ Only work on things that you can
control, and let the rest happen.

⊣ As you work on things you can
control, strive to ensure you're the
best in class by knowing how good
your competitors are and exceeding
their capabilities.

Weathering the Storm

❧ Readiness is perhaps the most important condition for responding to the opportunities that arise when market conditions change.

Finding the Flowers Among the Weeds

Lynda Gratton

Professor of Management Practice,
London Business School

THIS IS AN OLD STORY. I guess I must have been about twenty-six years old, and it was my very first year as a consultant. I was working for one of the big consulting practices, and I remember we all went over to

Weathering the Storm

Ireland to advise a company about its long-
term strategy.

Like any great consultants at that stage,
we asked everybody to get into a room, and
then we said to them, "Let's think about
what this organization could be like in ten
years' time." Over the space of a day, we
filled up about fifty flipcharts with all the
things that they could do for the future.
That was all great; we were really energetic,
and there were lots of ideas. Then, at the
end of the day, we stood in the middle of the
room and looked around. There must have
been two hundred things that we could do
in the future. And it struck me so forcibly
then—and actually it's been a huge learning
for me—that there just isn't any reason to
generate masses of ideas like that. What you
need to do is to know, of all the things that
you can really work on, what the one or two,
or maybe three or four things are that are
really going to make a difference.

I guess for me it's a bit like saying that
the garden is full of weeds, and some of the
weeds are actually flowers, but how do you

Finding the Flowers Among the Weeds

know which ones they are? Of all the things that you can do, which are the four things that will really make a difference to your organization?

Thinking back on that, the lesson for me was that you just have to focus. You absolutely have to focus. There are so many things you can do, so you have to just focus on the three or four things that will make a difference. But how do you do that? Well, those three or four things have to be very tightly aligned to what it is you're trying to do as an organization. They have to be aligned to your business strategy. They have to be big things; things that when employees look at them, they say, "I feel really excited about that; I feel really engaged in that."

I guess for me that the capacity to know what's a weed and what's a flower is really one of the most important things I ever learned. I've engaged with organizations many times in blue-sky thinking, but what I learned was that while having that many ideas was great, you had to find a way of synthesizing and filtering them down.

Weathering the Storm

And then the question is, how do you do that? I guess there are many ways, but the way that I learned to do it is by setting up a 3×3.

On one axis, I asked the executives, "How important do you think this is to the long-term success of this organization: very important, important, or not particularly important?" Then, we went back to the same items, and I said, "Thinking about that item, where are you now? Are you already doing that, have you started doing it, or haven't you even thought about it?" What we then got was this wonderful matrix: in the top right-hand corner were things that were very important for the long-term future but that people weren't doing anything about right now. We called those the areas of risk, and I think that was a great way of distilling from a large amount of data right down to things that are really important. And the reason they're really important is because they are things that are important to you for the future, but that you are not doing now.

TAKEAWAYS

⚔ Of all the things a company can work to achieve, it needs to identify what the three or four things are that will make the greatest difference.

⚔ Those three or four things have to be tightly aligned to what it is you're trying to do as an organization, they have to be aligned to your business strategy, and they have to be big enough to excite and engage employees.

⚔ Finding a way to filter and synthesize many ideas is an important way to determine which ideas are important now and which are important for the future.

Rising from the Ashes After a Crisis

Ping Fu

Chairman, President, and CEO, Geomagic

MY GREATEST CHALLENGE was in
the beginning of 2001, when the company
was given back to me and I became CEO.
I cofounded the company and, after raising
VC money, hired a management team.
We raised the money at a time when the

Weathering the Storm

Internet was very hot, and during that
time it was fashionable to bring in seasoned
managers; entrepreneurs usually are not
considered very good businesspeople.
So I stepped down from my role as CTO.

But two years down the road, the Internet
bubble crashed. As a founder of the company, I was left, basically, to steer the ship.
There was no one else in the management
team left at the time when the company was
going to die—or so everybody believed. Well,
the situation was far worse than I expected.
I was shell-shocked when the CEO told me,
"Ping, I have bad news for you. The company's going to run out of cash in three
months, and there's no chance that we're
going to survive. And more than that, I'm
leaving, and the VP of Sales is leaving, so
you are going to be left with the company.
You can decide whatever you want to do
with the company, since it's your baby."

I felt, first of all, a profound sense of
failure, because I was part of the management team, too. Their failure was my failure. That was my first reaction. The second
was fear: "Oh my God, I raised the money;

my own money, my family's money, the investors' money." The early people were friends of mine or students of my husband. They trusted me. Now I had to tell them that their money was down the drain and that they didn't have a job. I panicked.

But that didn't last very long. We had that meeting in the morning, and by the evening I'd told myself, "Well, the situation is what it is. There is nothing I can do by being shocked or being panicked. I've got to have a plan. I've got to do something."

The first thing is open communication; silence always brews distrust. So the very first thing I did was go to the board and tell them that I was willing to take over the company, stay with the company, and do whatever was best with what was left over. I would try to save the company, and if I could not I would try to sell the company so that they could get some investment back.

The second thing to do was to communicate with the employees and clearly tell them what the situation was, why I needed their help, and how much cash we had left. And then I told them I would survive because

Weathering the Storm

I have always been a survivor. I had gone through very tough situations when I was in China—in a crisis is when I shine. I asked them to stay with me, trust me, and help me through the difficult times. So you give them open communication, and you ask for help.

Other than that, I knew I needed to get cash and get cash fast. I couldn't worry about whether or not the business deal I was doing was the best deal or not. I couldn't worry about whether it was a right or wrong decision. Getting the deal to give me the cash was what was going to help us survive. I went after a large customer, which was Align Technology. They make Invisalign, the corrective braces for teeth, without wires and brackets. They were considering an IPO, and I offered them technology to make this possible.

Now if we had been in good condition, I probably could have negotiated a better deal that sustained revenue to this day. But I sold the technology to them for cash, so we got cash very quickly. They felt it was a fantastic deal for them. The technology was exactly what they needed to go public. They were happy, and I got what I needed to float the company: $2 million in three months.

Once we got the cash in place, morale was higher, and employees started to trust me more because I had delivered what I said I could deliver. By then we had not just three months of cash but a year of cash. The first strategy was: do not run out of cash. Then I hired a really good sales executive to help me sell the software. Knowing what caused the last team to fail, I had a better idea of who I needed to hire. In some ways, failure is never a failure; it can always serve to teach you what you need to do better next time. We were able to achieve positive cash flow at the end of the first year; profitability at the end of the second year; and by the end of the fifth year, we had grown more than 2,000 percent during the most difficult economic conditions.

I think to rise from the ashes you must keep a very cool, collected head because everybody's watching you. You must keep high integrity and remove any distrust that can possibly happen during the crisis because that's what's happening, emotions are running high—you must, must do that. And then you must be very clearheaded on a single strategy to survive and then execute on that. You don't have a lot of time to wander around.

TAKEAWAYS

- During a crisis, keep cool and collected in order to have a positive influence on the many people watching you.

- Maintain integrity and take proactive steps to remove distrust and fear when emotions are running high.

- Be very clearheaded on a single survival strategy and execute on it quickly and decisively.

Communicating Through Uncertain Times

Dame Barbara Stocking

Chief Executive, Oxfam

I'VE ALWAYS THOUGHT that communications with staff are important. After all, if you want people to go in the direction you're setting, they have to really know and understand it. But this came home to me most clearly when I was in the National Health Service.

In 1993 I became the Regional General Manager for the Oxford Regional Health Authority. And within a few months, the government had decided to change regional health authorities, bringing fourteen down to eight and also changing the whole way that they were working. That was very significant for all the staff because it meant that of two regions, Oxford and East Anglia, where there were eight hundred staff, we had to go down to about one hundred fifty. So, obviously, there were massive redundancies, real changes in jobs, and so on—a big change in its own right. On top of that, it was made even more difficult because the government couldn't decide how big it thought these regional bodies should be, which meant we couldn't actually give staff the new jobs, we couldn't go through the selection processes.

Now, for all staff that was clearly a very difficult time with all the uncertainty. From the beginning I tried to be honest and tell

them what was going on, but as the time
went by, that became increasingly important
rather than less important. It was very difficult at some points because I was appointed
the regional director of the combined
region, but for almost six months I was the
only person who had a job that was guaranteed into the future. Week after week
I would stand up in staff meetings at both
ends, in Oxford and Cambridge, and have
to say to staff, "I have no more news for you.
I don't know what's going to happen. Nothing has come through from the Treasury
about what size these regional offices are
going to be. So we can't get on with the
selection process; we can't get the certainty
that you want about jobs."

At the time, it was very hard to stand
in front of people and give those messages
week after week. But I was very pleased
at the end, when we'd been through all the
changes, and—it was about a year later—one
staff member who had stayed said to me,
"I have always thought that communications
with staff are important, but the thing that

Weathering the Storm

I learned from you was you have to do it
even when you have no news. You have to
keep standing there and telling people what
you do know, even if it isn't very much."

So I learned then, even when it's hard
going, you just have to keep communicating. The best method of communicating
is face to face. There's no doubt about that
at all. When I was in this big change process,
I would go and have staff meetings in the
offices in Oxford and Cambridge. It was up
to staff whether they came or not, but they
usually did because they wanted to know if
there was any news. Being there in person
is much the best way, but often you need to
reinforce that with something in writing so
people can take it away with them and think
about it and absorb what you are saying.
Because sometimes you're coming up with
some very difficult things for them to take
in at the time, especially if it means that
they're losing their jobs.

I can't overstate the importance of communication, especially in people organizations. Sometimes you have to do it in

writing, but if you can do it face to face, that's the best thing, because then people can really understand what you are trying to say to them.

TAKEAWAYS

- ⚑ As difficult times wear on, it becomes increasingly important, rather than less important, to communicate with staff, even when there is no news.

- ⚑ The best method of communication in difficult times is face to face.

- ⚑ Reinforce in-person communications with written communications that people can take away to review and absorb, especially when the news is challenging.

—◆◆◆—

When Your Brand Is Under Fire, Honesty Is the Best Policy

—◆◆◆—

Jimmy Wales

Founder, Wikipedia

WIKIPEDIA HAS ALWAYS grown very quickly. It was doubling in size every three to four months throughout its entire life until fairly recently, when it became so large that it began to taper off.

Weathering the Storm

There was one incident in particular in late 2005 that caused a pretty huge spike in growth, but it was unfortunately a very negative incident. Someone had vandalized the biography about John Seigenthaler, a journalist, by writing that he had been briefly suspected of something to do with the Kennedy assassination. It was completely false. In fact, Seigenthaler was a close friend of the Kennedy family; he was a pallbearer at Bobby Kennedy's funeral. He saw this about himself in Wikipedia and called me. We had it corrected within ten minutes, but the incorrect information had been in the article for four months.

I thought it was all settled. He seemed happy with the correction being done so promptly, but then he wrote a scathing editorial in *USA Today* that condemned us as irresponsible. This created an enormous sensation in the media.

For me this was an important incident because it was the first time when, for many people, Wikipedia had entered the cultural consciousness. For our community it was a seminal moment because a lot of people in the community who had not given thought to the power of Wikipedia started to think about it for the first time.

Before this, we thought of ourselves as a group of geeks off on the side of the Internet working on an open-source project. And in that moment, we, in a certain sense, transformed our thinking about ourselves into understanding and realizing that we're actually a very powerful and very influential media outlet.

That generated a whole set of new policies and new thinking in the communities about how we deal with errors and how we deal, in particular, with biographies of living people, which is always a problematic, difficult area for us. It was interesting to me too, because this was the first time I had been in the media spotlight in a negative way. The sudden negative attention led to a lot of on-the-job learning for me.

Ironically, the attention caused our traffic to triple in three months, so it wasn't all bad. I joke about that, but it also set off

these questions that we still face today.
How good is Wikipedia? Is it really reliable?
Is it irresponsible? What is it exactly? We are
dealing with the ramifications, all of which,
I think, started with the Seigenthaler story.
If it hadn't been that story, it would've been
another one.

One of the key things that we did at that
time and that we feel, even today, was very
effective for our brand image was to be
completely up front and honest about the
problems with our product. I am an evan-
gelist and a promoter; my job is to encourage people to participate in Wikipedia and
use it. So there's a real temptation—and
I think this is true of almost any company—
to hype your own product and to ignore
the weaknesses and failures. But we adopted
a very conscious strategy. When questions
about the quality of Wikipedia come
up, we try to set the bar for negativity.
In other words we say, yes, it's really big
and it's pretty good in parts; but there
are errors and there are problems. And
we're really passionate about the long-term

quality. We don't pretend to be perfect at
this time.

That strategy was a risky one, or we felt
it was risky at the time. In fact, there were a
few headlines that came out from negative
and critical press saying, "Even the founder
admits it's no good." Realistically, in the
long run, we felt like that was the right strategy because it helped people to see that we
were, in fact, responsible; that we actually
do care about quality; and that we're aware
of the problems and we're working to fix
them. That's more important for our brand
image than to pooh-pooh criticisms.

A lot of companies could learn from
that. Too often you see companies engaging
in dismissive hand-waving and spin control.
They'd be much better off to simply ac-
knowledge when a current product model
does have a lot of recalls—communicate
that they're doing their best, they're going
to recall them all, they're going to fix them,
and they're doing a redesign for the next
year's version—rather than downplay the
problem.

TAKEAWAYS

⚔ Crisis and any negative attention that results from it can precipitate significant growth and brand awareness, which will need to be managed.

⚔ How a company responds to negative attention and criticism can transform its perception of itself, as well as its identity in the marketplace.

⚔ Acknowledging product problems and deficiencies can create trust between a brand and its consumers.

———◆◆◆———

Communicate Directly and Honestly with Investors

———◆◆◆———

Blythe McGarvie

*CEO and Founder, Leadership
for International Finance*

SPEAKING TO AND persuading the investor community is one of the most critical skills the CFO has to learn. I know from my own experience that I did not have the exposure and personal opportunity to speak to investors until I became the CFO. I learned by watching former CFOs with whom I worked, and it really made me realize that there are two approaches. You can try and bully your way when you talk to the community, or another way is to be a little bit more honest and sometimes even show some of your failures. I'll give you an example.

As I started developing my own style of talking with investors, we had a major situation happen in 1993. I was the chief financial officer of Hannaford Brothers, which is a supermarket retail company based in the Northeast. We were *Fortune* 500, one of the little, stodgy, 2 percent, slow-growth companies; and this was the time of all the dot-com excitement. And we decided to test a concept called Hannaford HomeRuns, which was home delivery of groceries through Internet ordering. We were going along, testing this and talking about it, and all of a sudden, the worst thing imaginable happened. It was a spring day around

Communicate Directly and Honestly

noon, and the building where we housed
all the people working on Hannaford
HomeRuns.com collapsed. Luckily, it
was lunchtime, so many of the employees
were already gone. No one was killed.

What happened was that the building
right next door to our major center
was being torn down, and they tore down
a shared wall. All of a sudden, we had
no business. Here we had run with this
new concept. Instead of being a stodgy,
2 percent–growth company, we were
showing that we were growing business
in Boston. This warehouse was based right
outside Boston. We thought, "What's going
to happen? What's going to happen to, first
of all, our business? And second, how do
we convey to our investors and analysts that
what we thought was our future had just
disappeared?"

We talked about it, and we decided we'd
try something new. We'd try a DVD. Back
then, digital storytelling wasn't as popular
as perhaps it is now. It was the first time we
ever did this, and we found it incredibly

effective in speaking to our analysts. At that next quarterly meeting, we had created a DVD, and in it I showed some of the bad press, the TV news that talked about this collapsing building in Newton, Massachusetts.

We explained what happened, but we did something more than just show the problems; we also showed what we were going to do about it—how we were going to rebuild, how in some ways this actually was an opportunity. It allowed us to start with new processes. It allowed us to do some things that we had learned that didn't work in the old warehouse and restart. Luckily, we were honest. We were forthright. We explained the good and the bad. We said, "We're going to stick with this concept." And we did.

Hannaford HomeRuns.com continued to grow, slowly at first. We were a little bit behind our targets—a lot behind our targets—because of this delay and having to restart. But eventually, we ended up selling the business for a $100 million,

Communicate Directly and Honestly

and that really rewarded the shareholders who stood with us.

The lesson learned here is that you have to be direct with your investors, show the good and the bad, and you have to stay calm. You have to show all the facts, even the worst facts possible, but then explain, in a calm manner, what you are going to do about it. It's more than just "Here's the problem, and we are just going to fold." How you respond to a problem or an opportunity is much more important.

TAKEAWAYS

◄ Speaking to and persuading the investor community is one of the most critical skills the CFO has to learn.

◄ Be direct and honest with your investors, providing even the worst

Weathering the Storm

facts, but then calmly explaining what
actions you intend to take.

❧ How you respond to a problem or an
opportunity is much more important
than the problem itself.

———◆———

Riding Out a Recession

———◆———

Richard Santulli

Founder and CEO, NetJets

THE GREATEST CHALLENGE I had was back in 1989, when the recession occurred and interest rates went up 110 percent. At NetJets, we always buy the aircraft before we sell it. In other words, I don't wait to get eight people, eight-eighths on an airplane, and then go and take delivery of an airplane. We always buy it in advance, take delivery

from manufacturers, and then sell it.
I probably have forty or fifty airplanes
on order over a peak-year period. Those
are the commitments that we make.

So even in the early days back in 1986,
I made a commitment to take four airplanes
a year from Cessna, but in 1989–1990,
I only sold one-eighth. We were basically
broke. I had personally guaranteed all the
debt, which my attorneys told me I should
not have done. And I said that if the company was me and the company failed,
I should fail, too. And it was interesting,
because the lenders respected me for that.

At the time I owed $2 million. I had very
little revenue, and my CFO said we should
file for bankruptcy, which I said would
destroy the business. I wrote a letter to my
owners—and back in 1991, we had probably
about a hundred owners—apologizing
because every two years we would redo the
interior of our airplanes at our expense.
I wrote a letter to everyone saying that I was
very sorry that, because it had been difficult
from a financial point of view, we just

hadn't done the interiors. And almost to a one, I got a response back saying, "Gee, we didn't even know that, the service has been so great. You should have told us; we could have helped you out."

Then I realized that we had something with these hundred owners. Our business was correct; we were running the right program, although by the end I was paying for fuel with my credit card—that's how close it got. Luckily the recession ended.

Everybody now realizes that if you had an airplane you were trying to sell in 1989 and 1990, you couldn't sell it; there was no market. Zero. So all these guys I would meet with and ask, "Would you like to buy a quarter of an airplane?" would all say, "No, no. I own my airplane. I'm going to make money on it." So I would say, "Why would you want to spend a hundred dollars when you can spend twenty-five?" And it's even more, "Why would you want to spend ten million dollars when you could spend two and a half?" And they said, "Well, I'm going to make money on my airplane." But in

Weathering the Storm

1989 and 1990, not only couldn't you make money on them, you couldn't sell them. So it then became very fashionable to do fractional with us. And I don't have to use my credit card to buy fuel anymore! But that was a lesson.

Again, maybe I should have filed for bankruptcy? In retrospect, no. The professionals said I should, but I said I could always get a job. If the company went bad, I deserved not to have any money. And you know what? The lenders knew that, and they gave me a lot more slack than they would have someone else. I always told them what was going on, and with some of the vendors, like Pratt & Whitney, it was the same thing. If I didn't pay for some engines, they would be great. At First Aviation, where we buy our fuel now in Teterboro Airport, I didn't pay for any fuel for a while, and they would always say, "Rich, don't worry about it." And the companies that did that with me I still do business with. The ones that insisted I pay for catering with a credit card, we don't do any business with them.

TAKEAWAYS

- ⚐ Take realistic stock of your assets and direction during downturns to assess the true strength of your position and your strategy.

- ⚐ Being honest with your customers and constituents can provide significant advantages during a down economy.

- ⚐ Personal integrity and personal responsibility are key attributes for successfully weathering difficult times.

The Art of the Turnaround

Sir Gerry Robinson

Former Chairman, Allied Domecq

TURNING AROUND AN organization is probably one of the most exciting things you'll ever get to do. The very fact that it needs turning around means it's in trouble in the first place, and most people recognize that. So the advantage you have in a turn-around is that people know something has to happen. It's a very simple process: you get

to the people who run the various parts of
whatever it is that you've taken over, and you
get them to tell you what the issues are and
what they think they're going to do about it.
I promise you, within half an hour you
will know which of them actually know what
they're doing and which of them don't.

More often than not in that situation,
it's about changing the ones who don't know
what they're doing because you haven't got
much time; you are up against time. Never,
never, never carry out a reorganization
unless you're absolutely certain you're only
going to do it once, because there's nothing
worse than going through some kind of
terrible redundancy program and having to
come back to it again in three months' time.
Get in there quickly: the fact that it's a turnaround means the company is in trouble.

You have to look at what the issues are,
and you will nearly always have to change
some people. You're probably going to
have to take people out of the organization;
that's a fact of life. There's no point in having an organization go to the floor where

everybody loses. So you have to do something about it and do it quickly. Then get the people who are left behind rallied. Get them absolutely clear where you're going with it; get them excited about it.

Get the people who are going, out. Don't have them hanging around for six months; get them out. Pay them well, and don't be mean about the way you do the financial side. Be as generous as you sensibly can, but don't have them hanging around moaning for six months. Get them out. Then you'll need to rev up the group that remains again. They'll be up for it, because they've lived through this uncertainty for a very long time.

If you come in to do a turnaround and take nine months to do it, they're just thinking nothing is going to happen, they've settled down again—and then, bang! For heaven's sake, do it in six weeks, get on with it, and overdo it—and then rev up the people remaining. They will then really be up for it, and it's amazing how quickly things can start to happen.

Weathering the Storm

If you've got it right and it starts to work, the feeling's fantastic. People love it—they start to feel confident again, they start to feel that they can do things, they feel that decisions get made, they know where they are, they feel the mortgage is going to be paid. All of those things contribute to a circle, which is positive. It's amazing how effective that can be.

When I moved into Grand Met Contract Services, which was hugely loss making, it didn't take more than two days to pick out the three or four parts of the organization that were contributing most to the loss. Quite simply, I closed those three or four operations down—that was the first move. They were in organizations in parts of the world that were simply never going to make any money, in my view, yet they'd been allowed to go on because nobody had had the courage to say, "Look, I'm going to stop this." So it's stopping silly things.

Again, it sounds simple but it's amazing, particularly in a large organization, how often money is just wasted. Stop that; then look for the three or four things that really can do more than they're doing now. It's surprising how obvious that will be once you start to look at the numbers, start to talk to people. Concentrate on those three things ruthlessly—really drive those three things forward. Don't get caught up in the minutiae of other issues. Once you have the company on a stable footing, then you can start to talk about the smaller things that need balancing and checking.

However, it's the combined strength of those two things—stopping the really daft things that have to do with wasting money and really driving the things that can matter. In that organization, for example, we had one business that had two-and-a-half thousand customers. Well, if you get one thing right across two-and-a-half thousand customers, that's going to make a hell of a difference. I spent a lot of time concentrating on that business, and it did chip in very quickly. Then you get into the more boring part, which is making it work in a smooth way. That has to happen, but it doesn't have to happen first. The first thing to do is to stop the nonsense and concentrate on the real fast turnaround priorities; and you can spot them if you set out at the beginning to do so.

TAKEAWAYS

⚑ One advantage to turnarounds is that people recognize change has to happen.

⚑ In a turnaround, it's best to make staff reductions as quickly and fairly as possible and then immediately engage and energize the people left behind.

⚑ Once you've identified and adopted measures to eliminate financial waste and loss, concentrate ruthlessly on the two or three things you can do to drive the business forward successfully.

—◆—

Reinventing an Organization

Maurice Lévy

Chairman and CEO, Publicis Groupe

—◆—

ONE OF THE PROBLEMS we have as an
ad agency is the fact that not only must we
always deliver the best possible service to a
client, always use the best tools available,
and create some of the best programs, but—
as life is not easy—we also need to cope with
some of the constraints of our business. So
when there is a recession, we have to make

sure that we can cope with it; and when there is a pick-up we have to make sure that we don't have a huge rise in our cost. The best way to do that is constantly to reinvent ourselves.

In 1992 there was a very serious recession in France. Most—and when I say *most*, it was all—of our competitors had laid off something like 20 percent of their people. It was huge: 20 or 25 percent. There were companies or agencies that laid off much more; three hundred people, which is huge for an ad agency—perhaps 40 percent of the staff. And we thought, "These people are not responsible for this crisis; these people have created our wealth. To lay them off just because there is a recession seems unfair to them."

So we tried to create something. We created what we called "the economic revolution." This was a caucus over one month, every evening, where all the people in the agency met to try to find solutions. Then we came up with an idea: a referendum asking

Reinventing an Organization

if everyone was ready to cut their salaries,
starting with the CEO, in order to avoid
the layoffs. It worked. Not only did it work,
but we'd thought it would be necessary to
cut salaries for two years; after one year
we were able to reestablish the original
salaries.

So you see that by being innovative in the
way you manage the structure, changing it
and managing your people, you can find the
resources for more energy and more talent,
and create a culture that is shared by the
people. They feel good about the company,
they feel good about the way we care, and
obviously they work much more. And at the
end of the day, we win.

So never stabilize an organization;
never think that the organization is forever.
Always create an instability in the organization and make sure that you can move the
borders—from one department to another,
or one organization to another—very
quickly. Be fast in creating the opportunity
for reinventing yourself.

TAKEAWAYS

- ⚑ Reinventing your business is one of the soundest ways to cope with both downturns and upswings in the marketplace.

- ⚑ Look within the organization for creative solutions to challenging situations.

- ⚑ Embrace instability within your organization in order to enable reinvention.

Restoring Belief in a Struggling Business

Shelly Lazarus

Chairman and CEO, Ogilvy & Mather Worldwide

THE BIGGEST CHALLENGE that I ever faced in my business career was in 1991. Three years before, I had left Ogilvy Advertising to run Ogilvy Direct, which was the agency's direct marketing arm. And in the intervening years since I went to Direct,

which actually was a relatively new company
and very, very successful, the advertising
agency in New York had gone through some
really, really tough times. The company was
suffering, people were leaving, clients were
leaving, and revenue was going down.

It was at this moment that I was asked to
return to the advertising agency in New
York and to run it. I came back, and I dis-
covered many of the people I had worked
with before. But they were now discouraged,
demoralized; life was grim. Everyone was
pessimistic. I actually remember being in a
room with them the first week I came back,
because I called all the leaders together, just
to talk about where we were. And their bodies were almost contorted. You know, there
was a physical aspect to being depressed
and demoralized. They were sitting at odd
angles. And I actually said to them "I recognize you all, because I worked with you
for years, but you don't look as good as
you used to look."

For the first six months, I used to have
this recurring nightmare—seriously—that
I got to the office one morning and all the

Restoring Belief in a Struggling Business

clients had left and all the people had left. And I was all alone in this place. So, what do you do? You turn the lights out. But the truth was that everyone had their résumés on the street, and all the clients were wondering whether they should stay at Ogilvy, because it was falling apart.

I realized that the first thing I needed to do was restore a belief in the people themselves, the ones who were at the agency, because if they all left, we were nowhere. And I had to give them hope. The reason they were so discouraged was, they didn't see how they could turn this ship around. And here again, I learned something. I did it instinctively, and I learned how important it was. If you say to an individual, "Your job is to turn around this company," they say, "Too hard, too hard! Impossible! Not at this stage." But if you divide the task up and make the challenge something that people think they can do—so you say to an individual, "I don't need you to turn around Ogilvy New York. All I need you to do is to get us some good work on Maxwell House"—then the person says, "Oh! I could do that."

Weathering the Storm

But to get people to the point of believing "I can do this" is crucial to any turnaround. You have to divide the task into bite-sized pieces, and you have to do anything you can to create a little bit of success. In my instance, I went in, and I talked with two or three former clients who had gone to other places. I sat down with them, and I said, "Give us a shot. Give me an assignment. I'll do it, and for not a lot of money, but I just need some new things. I need to show that business is coming into Ogilvy. So you're in a lucky place today, because I'm willing to do it for a little money. I have everything riding on it, so I'm going to give it every-thing I have to make this work successful."

And so slowly, slowly, we got some new clients. Slowly, slowly, we got some wonder-ful advertising. Slowly, slowly, we started to have a little bit of success. That gave me all the motivation to continue on. And then once you get it started, momentum builds. Momentum is a wonderful thing. It's a ter-rible thing in the downward spiral, because there's momentum there, too. But you also know if you can just start a little bit of success and get people believing, then the momentum builds and builds. We turned it around.

It didn't take that long. I'd say it took a year to get it going in the positive direction. And the satisfaction, when it actually starts to turn, is enormous. I can say it now: it was worth all those dark days. Because it's not the business success; it's that you did it with a group of people who stayed with you, who believed, who gave it everything they had as well. And then you get to a point where you can look at each other and think, "My God, we did it!"

TAKEAWAYS

✄ Leading people to the point of believing "I can do this" is crucial to any turnaround.

Weathering the Storm

✠ Rather than assign or take on over-whelming challenges, divide tasks into actions that individuals feel they can successfully execute.

✠ Do anything you can to create and build on small successes, which will gradually generate enough momentum to move the business in a positive direction.

Erroll Davis Jr. is the former Chairman of Alliant
Energy Corporation. Currently, he is the Chancellor of the University System of Georgia.

Mr. Davis worked in the energy industry for
over twenty-five years. He joined Wisconsin Power
and Light Company in 1978, became CEO ten
years later, and also served as President until 1998.
Following the merger of Wisconsin Power and Light
with Alliant Energy in 1998, Mr. Davis became
President and CEO of Alliant Energy. He stayed
in the role of CEO until June 2005 and remained
as Chairman of the company until 2006, when
he stepped down. Mr. Davis also served as CEO of
Alliant Energy Resources, Inc. and Iowa Power and
Light Co. (or their predecessor companies) following the merger.

In February 2006 Mr. Davis took office as
Chancellor of the University System of Georgia,
where he is responsible for the state's 35 public
colleges and universities, approximately 283,000
students, 40,000 faculty and staff, and an annual
budget of $6.1 billion. The University System also
has administrative responsibility for the Georgia

About the Contributors

Public Library Service, which manages the state's 58 public library systems.

Mr. Davis is a member of the board of directors of General Motors, BP Plc. and Union Pacific Corp., and serves on the National Commission on Energy Policy along with numerous professional associations and civic organizations. He is a former member of the U.S. Olympic Committee Board (2004–2008).

Ping Fu is Chairman, President, and CEO of Geomagic. She cofounded Geomagic and has led its growth from a start-up to worldwide leader in the digital shape sampling and processing (DSSP) industry.

Before starting Geomagic, Ms. Fu was Director of Visualization at the National Center for Supercomputing Applications, where she initiated and managed the NCSA Mosaic software project that led to Netscape and Internet Explorer. She has more than twenty years of software industry experience in database, networking, geometry processing, and computer graphics. Ms. Fu is a respected thought leader and frequent keynote speaker at international conferences.

Ms. Fu has received numerous awards for her management achievements, including the Ernst & Young Entrepreneur of the Year for the Carolinas, worldwide "Fast 50" executive by *Fast Company* magazine, Entrebizneur of the Year by *Business Leader* magazine, and *Triangle Business Journal*'s Women in

About the Contributors

Business, Class of 2005. In 2005, she was named Entrepreneur of the Year by *Inc.* magazine, the leading publication for American entrepreneurs.

Ms. Fu holds graduate and postgraduate degrees in computer science and Chinese literature, and is an adjunct professor at Duke University.

Lynda Gratton is the Professor of Management Practice at the London Business School. In this role she directs the school's executive program Human Resource Strategy in Transforming Organizations. She is considered one of the world's authorities on people in organizations and actively advises companies across the world.

A trained psychologist, Ms. Gratton worked for the global airline British Airways for several years as an occupational psychologist, and then became Director of HR Strategy at PA Consulting Group. From 1992 to 2002, she led the Leading Edge Research Consortium.

Professor Gratton's book *Living Strategy*, originally published in 2000, has been translated into more than fifteen languages and rated by U.S. CEOs as one of the most important books of the year. Her book *The Democratic Enterprise* was described by *Financial Times* as a work of important scholarship. Her latest book, published in 2007, is *Hot Spots: Why Some Teams, Workplaces, and Organizations Buzz with Energy and Others Don't*.

In 2005 Ms. Gratton was appointed Director of the Lehman Centre for Women in Business.

About the Contributors

In 2007, she was included in the *Times'* list of the top fifty business thinkers in the world.

William Harrison retired as Chairman, Director, and CEO of JPMorgan Chase & Co. in December 2006. Mr. Harrison held this title since November 2001.

From January 2001 until that time, he held the position of President and CEO. Prior to the merger with J.P. Morgan & Co., Inc., Mr. Harrison had been Chairman and CEO of the Chase Manhattan Corporation, a position he assumed in January 2000.

He had held the same responsibilities at the Chemical Bank prior to its merger with Chase in 1996. In 1978 he moved to London to take responsibility for the bank's U.K. business and in 1982 was promoted to Division Head of Europe. Mr. Harrison returned to the United States in 1983 to run the U.S. corporate division, and was put in charge of the bank's global Banking and Corporate Finance group three years later.

Mr. Harrison is a Director for Cousins Properties, Inc. and has been a Director for Merck & Co. since 1999.

Shelly Lazarus is the Chairman and CEO of brand agency Ogilvy & Mather Worldwide.

Ms. Lazarus has been with the agency network for more than three decades. After rising through the ranks of account management and playing a pivotal role on many of Ogilvy & Mather's signature accounts—including American Express, Kraft, and Unilever—she left the general agency to become the General Manager for Ogilvy & Mather Direct in the United States.

Her success there led to positions of increasing responsibility, from President of Ogilvy & Mather Advertising in New York in 1991, to President of Ogilvy North America three years later. Just one year later, she became CEO and President of Ogilvy & Mather Worldwide. She was named CEO in 1996 and became Chairman in 1997.

Ms. Lazarus was named Woman of the Year in 2002 by the Direct Marketing Association. She has appeared in *Fortune* magazine's annual ranking of America's 50 Most Powerful Women in Business for ten years since the list's inception in 1998. She was also the first woman to receive Columbia Business School's Distinguished Leader in Business Award.

Ms. Lazarus serves on the boards of several corporate, philanthropic, and academic institutions: General Electric, Merck, New York Presbyterian Hospital, American Museum of Natural History, Committee Encouraging Corporate Philanthropy, World Wildlife Fund, and the Board of Overseers of Columbia Business School, where she received her MBA in 1970.

Maurice Lévy is the Chairman and CEO of Publicis Groupe, one of the world's largest advertising and media services conglomerates. With headquarters in Paris and offices in more than one hundred countries, Publicis is responsible for such brands as Cadbury, Coca-Cola, General Mills, and Procter & Gamble. Total sales for 2007 were $6,875 million.

Mr. Lévy joined Publicis in 1971. He was given responsibility for its data processing and information technology systems. However, he moved swiftly up the organization, being appointed Corporate Secretary in 1973, Managing Director in 1976, and Chairman of Publicis Conseil in 1984.

He was appointed Chairman and CEO of Publicis in 1988.

Mr. Lévy sits on the board of the World Economic Foundation.

J. W. Marriott Jr. is Chairman and CEO of Marriott International, Inc., one of the world's largest lodging companies. His leadership spans more than fifty years, and he has taken Marriott from a family restaurant business to a global lodging company with more than twenty-eight hundred properties in sixty-eight countries and territories.

During high school and college, Mr. Marriott was employed by the Hot Shoppes restaurant chain, where he worked in a variety of positions.

He joined Marriott full-time in 1956 and soon afterward took over management of the company's first hotel. Mr. Marriott became Executive Vice President of the company and then, in 1964, became its President. He was elected CEO in 1972 and Chairman in 1985.

Mr. Marriott serves on the boards of Sunrise Assisted Living and the National Urban League and is Director of the Naval Academy Endowment Trust and the National Geographic Society. He is a member of the U.S. Travel and Tourism Promotional Advisory Board, the World Travel & Tourism Council, and the National Business Council.

He also chairs the President's Export Council and the Leadership Council of the Laura Bush Foundation for America's Libraries.

Blythe McGarvie is the CEO and Founder of Leadership for International Finance, a private consulting firm offering a global perspective for clients to achieve profitable growth and providing leadership seminars for corporate and academic groups. In addition, Ms. McGarvie currently serves on the boards of Accenture, Pepsi Bottling Group, St. Paul Travelers, and Wawa.

Prior to founding LIF, Ms. McGarvie was based in Paris as the Executive Vice President and Chief Financial Officer of BIC Group, one of the world's leading manufacturers of convenient disposable products. Previously, she served as Senior Vice President and CFO of Hannaford Brothers Co., a *Fortune* 500 supermarket retailer that was acquired by the Delhaize Group in 1999.

Before joining Hannaford, she was Chief Administrative Officer—Pacific Rim, Sara Lee

About the Contributors

Corporation. In that capacity, she was responsible for the finance, strategy, information systems, and human resources functions for the personal product business in Asia, Australia, and South America, where she grew the division from $124 million to $600 million in sales over a three-year period ending in 1994.

Ms. McGarvie is a Certified Public Accountant and earned an MBA degree from Kellogg Graduate School of Management at Northwestern University. She received the Kellogg Graduate School of Management Schaffner Award, presented to alumni who are preeminent in their field and who provided outstanding service to Kellogg. In 2003, she was appointed as Senior Fellow of The Kellogg Innovation Network.

Sir Michael Rake is Chairman of BT Group, Plc. He is Chairman of the UK Commission for Employment and Skills, as well as Director of Barclays Plc., McGraw-Hill, Inc., and the Financial Reporting Council. He is also Chairman of the private equity oversight group, the Guidelines Monitoring Committee.

From May 2002 to September 2007, Sir Michael was Chairman of KPMG International. Prior to his appointment as Chairman of KPMG International, he was Chairman of KPMG in Europe and Senior Partner of KPMG in the United Kingdom.

He joined KPMG in 1974 and worked in Continental Europe before transferring to the Middle

About the Contributors

East to run the practice for three years in 1986. He transferred to London in 1989, became a member of the U.K. Board in 1991, and had a number of leadership roles in the United Kingdom before being elected U.K. Senior Partner in 1998.

Sir Michael is also a Vice President of the RNIB, a member of the Board of the TransAtlantic Business Dialogue, a member of the CBI International Advisory Board, the Chartered Management Institute, the Department of Trade and Industry's U.S./U.K. Regulatory Taskforce, the Advisory Council for Business for New Europe, the Ethnic Minority Employment Taskforce, The School of Oriental and African Studies Advisory Board, the Advisory Board of the Judge Institute at the University of Cambridge, and the Global Advisory Board of the Oxford University Centre for Corporate Reputation. He is Senior Adviser for Chatham House and an Association Member of BUPA.

Sir Gerry Robinson is the former Chairman of Allied Domecq, an international company that operated spirits and wine companies and quick service restaurants.

After leaving college at age seventeen, Sir Gerry planned to become a priest. Instead, in 1965, he joined Matchbox (a division of Mattel, Inc.), a company he stayed with for nine years before moving to Lex Service Group, Plc.

In 1980 he joined Grand Metropolitan as the Finance Director of the U.K. Coca-Cola business. He became Managing Director in 1982 and then took up the mantle of CEO of Grand Met's Contract Services Division. In 1987 he led the management buyout of the business from Grand Metropolitan.

He joined Granada, Plc. as CEO in 1991, latterly overseeing the company's takeover of Forte Hotels in 1996. He was then instrumental in the merger between Granada Group and Compass Group, Plc. in 2000. He retired from Granada in 2001 and became Chairman of Allied Domecq, Plc. a year later. He stood down as Chairman after Allied Domecq's takeover by Pernod Ricard.

Sir Gerry was awarded a knighthood in the 2003 New Year's Honours for Services to the Arts and Business.

Richard T. Santulli is Founder and CEO of NetJets Inc., the company that has revolutionized private and corporate business jet travel through fractional aircraft ownership.

From 1969 to 1979, Mr. Santulli was an investment banker with Goldman, Sachs & Co., where he held various managerial positions, including Vice President of Investment Banking and President of Goldman Sachs Leasing Corporation. He earned his BA and MA degrees in applied mathematics and operations research from Brooklyn Polytechnic Institute.

In 1986 Mr. Santulli developed the successful NetJets program. In 1996 he introduced the NetJets Europe program, and in 1999 he inaugurated

About the Contributors

NetJets Middle East. He has plans to expand the NetJets fractional aircraft ownership program into South America and the Asia/Pacific countries to provide a worldwide network of NetJets aircraft.

Mr. Santulli is a Director of the Andre Agassi Charitable Foundation.

Sir Nick Scheele is the former President and CEO of Ford Motor Company. He was appointed to the Board of British American Tobacco, Plc. as a Director in February 2005. He became the Senior Independent Non-Executive Director in May 2008 and is a member of the Audit, Corporate Social Responsibility, Nominations, and Remuneration Committees.

Sir Nick was President and CEO of Ford Motor Company from October 2001 until his retirement in February 2005. He had a long and distinguished career with Ford, during which time he held a number of significant positions including Chairman of Ford Europe, Chairman and CEO of Jaguar Cars Limited, and President of Ford of Mexico.

Sir Nick is a former Chancellor of Warwick University and serves as a Director of Caparo Plc. Sir Nick was awarded his knighthood in 2001.

Dame Barbara Stocking is the Chief Executive, Oxfam GB, an organization working to overcome poverty and suffering around the world.

Dame Barbara is a former member of the top management team of the National Health Service

About the Contributors

(NHS). In her eight years there, she worked as Regional Director, and more recently she served as Director of the Modernization Agency, charged with modernizing the NHS. She has broad experience of healthcare systems, policy, and practice, including periods at the World Health Organization in West Africa and the National Academy of Sciences in the United States.

Dame Barbara joined Oxfam as Director in May 2001. Her interests have been in bringing about change and development in healthcare. This is something she has brought to Oxfam's work in fighting poverty through humanitarian relief, development work, and advocacy.

Dame Barbara was awarded the title Dame Commander of the British Empire in June 2008 for humanitarian service.

Jimmy Wales is the Founder of Wikipedia, the free open-content encyclopedia.

From 1994 to 2000, Mr. Wales was the Research Director at Chicago Options Associates, a futures and options trading firm in Chicago. In 2000 he started the open-content encyclopedia Nupedia. In 2001 he founded Wikipedia, a free, online encyclopedia that anyone can edit.

Mr. Wales is the Chairman of Wikimedia Foundation Inc., a nonprofit charitable organization dedicated to encouraging the growth, development, and distribution of free, multilingual content. He is the Cofounder of Wiki, Inc., a wiki farm

that includes a collection of wikis on different topics, all hosted on the same site.

He is a Fellow at the Berkman Center for Internet and Society at Harvard Law School and a Director of Creative Commons, a nonprofit licensing
organization.

In 2006 Mr. Wales was named as one of *Time*
magazine's people who shape our world, and
in 2007 he was named as a *Forbes* magazine Web
celebrity.

⊰ ACKNOWLEDGMENTS ⊱

First and foremost, a heartfelt thanks goes to all of the executives who have candidly shared their hard-won experience and battle-tested insights for the *Lessons Learned* series.

Secondly, a special thanks to Mark Thompson for helping us frame the issues in a thoughtful and provocative Foreword, and for his continued involvement with 50 Lessons.

Angelia Herrin at Harvard Business Publishing has consistently offered unwavering support, good humor, and counsel from the inception of this ambitious project.

Brian Surette and David Goehring provided invaluable editorial direction, perspective, and encouragement, particularly for this second series. Many thanks to the entire HBP team of designers, copyeditors, and marketing professionals who helped bring this series to life.

Much appreciation goes to Jennifer Lynn and Christopher Benoît for research and diligent attention to detail, and to Roberto de Vicq de Cumptich for his imaginative cover designs.

Finally, thanks to our fellow cofounder James MacKinnon and the entire 50 Lessons team for

Acknowledgments

the tremendous amount of time, effort, and
steadfast support of this project.

—Adam Sodowick and Andy Hasoon
Directors and Cofounders, 50 Lessons